The Stravinsky Piano Collection
14 Pieces

BOOSEY & HAWKES

DISTRIBUTED BY

HAL•LEONARD®
CORPORATION
7777 W. BLUEMOUND RD. P.O. BOX 13819 MILWAUKEE, WI 53213

www.boosey.com
www.halleonard.com

Igor Stravinsky

(1882–1971)

Igor Feodorovich Stravinsky was born in Oranienbaum (now Lomonosov), a Baltic resort near St Petersburg, on June 5, (June 17, New Style) 1882, the third son of Feodor Stravinsky, one of the principal basses at the Maryinsky (later Kirov) Theatre in St Petersburg. Stravinsky's musical education began with piano lessons at home when he was ten; he later studied law at St Petersburg University and music theory with Fyodor Akimenko and Vassily Kalafati. His most important teacher, though, was Nikolay Rimsky-Korsakov, with whom he studied informally from the age of twenty, taking regular lessons from 1905 until 1908.

Although Stravinsky's first substantial composition was a Symphony in E-flat, written in 1906 under the tutelage of Rimsky-Korsakov, it was *The Firebird*, a ballet commissioned by Sergei Diaghilev and premiered by his Ballets Russes in Paris in 1910, that brought Stravinsky into sudden international prominence. In the next year he consolidated his reputation with *Pétrouchka*, like *The Firebird* a transformation of something essentially Russian into a work of surprising modernity. Stravinsky's next major score — a third ballet commission from Diaghilev — is one of the major landmarks in the history of music: the blend of melodic primitivism and rhythmic complexity in *The Rite of Spring* marked the coming of modernism in music and was met with a mixture of astonishment and hostility. Stravinsky, now a Swiss resident, became established, as the most radical composer of the age.

A rapid succession of works — *The Nightingale*, an opera, in 1914, *Renard* in 1915, *The Soldier's Tale* in 1918, the *Symphonies of Wind Instruments* two years after that — all reinforced his aesthetic dominance. The explicitly Russian flavor of his music — played out in the *Symphonies of Wind Instruments* (1920), the opera buffa *Mavra* (1922) and *Les Noces* (1923), for four solo voices, chorus and an orchestra consisting of four pianos and percussion — now gave way to a more refined neo-classicism, beginning with the ballet *Pulcinella* (1920), for which Stravinsky went back to the music of Pergolesi, reworking it into something completely personal.

1920 was also the year that Stravinsky settled in France, taking French citizenship in 1934. Stravinsky expected to be elected to a vacant seat in the Académie française following Dukas' death in 1935, and felt rebuffed when Florent Schmitt was elected in his stead. His ties to his adopted homeland were further loosened when, in a mere eight months, from November 1938, Stravinsky suffered the deaths of his daughter Lyudmilla, aged only 29, his mother and then his wife (and cousin) Catherine (*née* Nossenko); faced with an imminent war in Europe, Stravinsky and his second-wife-to-be Vera Sudeikin (*née* de Bosset) emigrated to the United States. After a year spent on the East Coast, including a stint as a lecturer at Harvard University, he and Vera soon settled in California, which they were to make their home for the rest of their lives.

Pulcinella turned out to be only the first of many works in which, over the next two decades, Stravinsky subdued the music of the past to his own purposes, among them the 'divertimento' *The Fairy's Kiss*, derived from Tchaikovsky, and the ballet *Apollon Musagète*, both premiered in 1928. Two choral-orchestral works — the oratorio *Oedipus Rex* (1927) and the *Symphony of Psalms* (1930) — showed that he could also work on an epic scale; and it was not long before he tackled a purely orchestral *Symphony in C* (1938), which was followed within four years by the *Symphony in Three Movements*. With *Perséphone* (1934), *Jeu de Cartes* (1936) and *Orpheus* (1946), the series of ballets also continued, generally in collaboration with George Balanchine, a partnership as important to dance in the twentieth century as Tchaikovsky's and Petipa's had been in the nineteenth. Stravinsky's neo-classical period culminated in 1951 in his three-act opera *The Rake's Progress*, to a libretto by W. H. Auden and Chester Kallman.

One of the most unexpected stylistic volte-faces in modern music came in 1957, with the appearance of the ballet *Agon*; Stravinsky himself conducted its premiere at a 75th-birthday concert. Hitherto he had ignored Schoenbergian serialism, but in 1952 he began to study Webern's music intensely and *Agon* was the first work in which he embraced serialism wholeheartedly, though the music that resulted was entirely his own — indeed, it has a formal elegance that he seemed to have been trying to capture in his neo-classical period. The chief works from Stravinsky's late serial flowering are *Threni*, for six solo voices, chorus and orchestra (1958), *The Flood*, a 'musical play for soloists, chorus and orchestra' (1962), the 'sacred ballad' *Abraham and Isaac* (1963), *Variations for Orchestra* (1964) and *Requiem Canticles* (1966).

Stravinsky was also active as a performer of his own music, initially as a pianist but increasingly as a conductor. The first among contemporary composers to do so, he left a near-complete legacy of recordings of his own music, released then on CBS and now to be found on Sony Classical. His conducting career continued until 1967, when advancing age and illness forced him to retire from the concert platform. His tenuous grasp on life finally broke on April 6, 1971, in New York, and his body was flown to Venice for burial on the island of San Michele, near to the grave of Diaghilev.

Contents

iv   *Notes from the original publications*

Chant du Rossignol
1   1. La fête au palais de l'empereur de Chine
14   2. Les deux Rossignols
25   3. Maladie et guérison de l'empereur de Chine

36   Chorus from the Prologue to 'Boris Godunov'

Les cinq doigts
39   1. Andantino
40   2. Allegro
42   3. Allegretto
43   4. Larghetto
44   5. Moderato
45   6. Lento
46   7. Vivo
48   8. Pesante

Four Études
50   1
54   2
61   3
64   4

72   Fragment des symphonies pour instruments à vent à la mémoire de Achille-Claude Debussy

75   Piano Rag-Music

84   Polka

Serenade in A
86   Hymn
90   Romanza
94   Rondoletto
100   Cadenza Finale

Sonata
104   1
111   2
116   3

122   Souvenir d'une marche boche

124   Tango

Trois mouvements de Pétrouchka
129   1. Danse Russe
136   2. Chez Pétrouchka
144   3. La semaine grasse

166   Valse

170   Valse pour les enfants

Notes from the original publications

ARGUMENT from *Chant du Rossignol*

THE PLOT

1.
Celebration in the Chinese Emperor's Palace

"Extraordinary preparations were made" to welcome the singing bird. "The porcelain walls and floors gleamed in the light of a hundred thousand gold lamps. The hallways were trimmed with the brightest of flowers, to which were attached the loveliest tiny bells. All the comings and goings stirred breezes up and down the halls, making all the bells ring..." The Nightingale is placed on a golden perch, and a CHINESE MARCH marks the Emperor's entrance.

2.
The Two Nightingales

"The Nightingale sang so sweetly that tears came to the Emperor's eyes..." "Even the footmen and valets seemed deeply pleased, which was remarkable since they are the hardest people to please..." Envoys from the Japanese Emperor arrive bearing the mechanical Nightingale. "Once the mechanism was wound, it began to sing a melody and moved its tail, which glinted with gold and silver..." "It had as much success as the other bird and, in addition, was beautiful to behold..." "But where was the real Nightingale? It had flown out the window unobserved..." We hear the song of the fisherman, who has been reunited with his friend.

3.
The Chinese Emperor's Illness and Recovery

"The poor Emperor could barely breathe. He opened his eyes and saw Death wearing his gold crown upon its head, with the Emperor's saber in one hand and his magnificent banner in the other. Wherever the Emperor looked, strange faces appeared in the folds of the heavy velvet curtains... the faces of his good and evil deeds... The things they said made perspiration run down his forehead..." "The mechanical bird would not sing. Then, the little Nightingale's song could be heard near the window. Thanks to its magical voice, the visions became paler and paler... Death itself listened and said, 'Sing on, little Nightingale...' Death gave up each treasure in exchange for a song... and drifted out the window like a cold, white mist..." "The Emperor fell into a peaceful, curative sleep. The sun was shining through the window when he awoke, strong and fully recovered." FUNERAL MARCH, members of the court enter to see their late Emperor one last time... And as they stand there astonished, the Emperor simply wishes them "Good morning!" – The fisherman, whom the bird has rejoined, sings his song again.

(Excerpted from Andersen's story, "*The Nightingale*")

The Song of the Nightingale was first performed on December 6, 1919 by the Suisse Romande orchestra under the direction of Ernest Ansermet. [Translated from the French for this edition.]

EDITOR'S PREFACE from *Serenade in A*

In the 1920s, when most of Stravinsky's piano music was written, the composer took a very strong stand against 'over-interpretation', and also against the 'expressivity' of the late 19th and early 20th century music, which had often led to an excess of indications of dynamic and expressive nuances. He therefore limited such indications in his own scores to an absolute minimum.

But what had seemed to him a legitimate protection against possible abuses soon revealed serious disadvantages. Afraid of betraying the composer's intentions or allowing their own initiative to take over, performers often gave the impression that a 'truthful' Stravinsky performance was a colorless one. This was by no means the composer's own view.

I have had the unique privilege of learning all Stravinsky's piano music under his guidance and direction, and maintained a longtime professional contact with him. It seemed to me that I had an imperative obligation to transmit this precious tradition to future pianists and musicians.

Fifty years of personal experience in playing and teaching these works and lecturing about them made me aware of the need for a practical performing edition of Stravinsky's piano compositions. Such is the purpose of the present edition.

EDITOR'S REPORT from *Serenade in A*

The edition is based on the following sources:

1. First edition (FE): Igor Stravinsky/Sérénade en la/en quatre mouvements/pour Piano/[…] Propriété de l'Editeur pour tous pays/Edition Russe de Musique/(Russischer Musikverlag/Berlin/[…] Paris). RMV 468.

2. Renewed edition (RE): Igor Stravinsky/Sérénade en la/Serenade in A/en quatre mouvements/pour Piano. Edited by/Albert Spalding/New York. Copyright 1926 by Edition Russe de Musique (Russischer Musikverlag) for all countries. Copyright assigned 1947 to Boosey & Hawkes Inc., New York, U.S.A. B&H 16303.

3. Gramophone recording (GR) made by the composer in Paris in 1934 for the Columbia Gramophone Company; originally released on two 78rpm discs, the recording has been reissued in the USA on a long playing disc by Seraphim (Great Recordings of the Century, Mono 60183).

FE carries on the first page of music the same credit to Albert Spalding, the distinguished violinist, as does RE. It was apparently motivated more by considerations of copyright than of musicological authenticity.

Stravinsky's dynamics and other signs of interpretation in FE and RE are sparse and sometimes misleading. For instance, in the opening Hymn, most of the dynamic indications are confined to the first page. In the remaining three movements, the player is almost without guidance as to dynamics. With the notable exception of the minutely marked Romanza, the phrasing marks are equally sparse.

EDITOR'S REPORT (continued)

The following is a list of all dynamic and pedal marks in FE and RE:

Hymn:

m.1:	*f*
m.7:	*p*
m.11:	<
m.15:	*f*
m.20:	*p*
m.27:	<
m.31:	*p* (should be on m.30)
m.51:	*f*
m.52:	*p*
m.65:	*p sub.*
m.76:	> *p secco*

Romanza:

m.4: (L.H.) *f secco* / *sord.*

m.8: (L.H.) *Ped............*

m.75: (L.H.)

Rondoletto:

m.27:	*sf*
m.86:	*sub. meno f*
m.88:	*sf sub.*

Cadenza Finale:

No dynamics indicated in the whole movement. Only a hint at the very end (m.105 & 106):

appena

Ped.

In elaborating or amending these markings I have relied more on my recollection of Stravinsky's own practice than on evidence of GR. Indeed in certain cases GR seems at odds with the musical sense. The following dynamics in GR are certainly questionable:

Rondoletto:

m.28:	*p sub.*
m.68:	*p sub.*
m.89–123:	*mf*

Cadenza Finale:

m.58:	*mf*
m.70:	*p sub.*

With regard to tempi GR tends to confirm my recollection in the following important respects:

Hymn:

FE/RE ♩. = 56
GR ♩. = 68

Romanza:

FE/RE/GR ♪ = 96

Rondoletto:

FE/RE ♩ = 92
GR ♩ = 104

Cadenza Finale:

FE/RE ♩ = 84
GR ♩ = 96

In anything pertaining to phrasing, the picture is more complicated, and less susceptible to summary description. Indeed, there is no substitute for a close comparison of all the available sources, including, of course, GR, which sheds light on several passages in this present edition: see Rondoletto, m.1, mm.42–43, mm.98–99.

Soulima Stravinsky
Urbana, Illinois
March 1978

FOREWORD from *The Short Piano Pieces*

PIANO RAG-MUSIC

Composed at Morges, Switzerland, in 1919.

♩ = 144 is the composer's own marking. The editor's parentheses do not mean to challenge this tempo but merely to indicate that the given metronome indication is a general time reference rather than a musical yardstick.

The interpretation of Jazz music allows for a certain flexibility, a seemingly relaxed negotiation of rhythmic pulsation. Such approach, it seems, would be adequate for PIANO RAG-MUSIC which style, akin to early Jazz, sought to portray and underline most of its typical features.

TANGO

Composed at Hollywood, California, in 1940.

When he was composing TANGO, Stravinsky intended from the outset a piece for instrumental ensemble. However, the orchestral version was not to materialize for a few years. In the meantime the music was set in an elaborate sketch in which almost every note of the orchestration was made to fit onto the two staves of a piano solo arrangement. In this form it was published, and though it was not exactly a composition for the piano, the nature of its music, the conciseness of its texture and clarity of the piano layout made it a keyboard piece in its own right.

N.B. The editor has slightly modified the right hand part in measures 27, 28 and 29 for easier command of the prevailing melodic line.

LES CINQ DOIGTS (The Five Fingers)

8 easy tunes on 5 notes.

Composed at Garches (near Paris) in the winter of 1920–1921.

These eight pieces intended for children's repertoire all have in common a little device whereby (according to the composer's own description) "the five fingers of the right hand once on the keys, remain in the same place sometimes even for the whole length of the piece, while the left hand which is destined to accompany the melody, executes a pattern either harmonic or contrapuntal of the utmost simplicity." He further adds in the same passage of his autobiography: "I found it rather amusing, with these much restricted means, to try to awaken in the child a taste for melodic design in combination with a rudimentary accompaniment."

In 1925 Stravinsky made a recording of this little suite. It was never released but I had ample opportunity to study it in the composer's archives. I vividly remember the subtle choice of nuances and I particularly noted the timing he used in his interpretation. No printed symbol can fully translate the poetic mood of this unique performance, but the present edition has at least attempted to make clearer the composer's intentions. Thus metronomic data, dynamics and phrase markings, as well as some fingering suggestions may be regarded merely as guidelines toward an interpretation consistent with his wishes.

No. 6, LENTO, measure 9: The sustained middle D, (Not in the original edition) was suggested by the composer at a later time.

No. 7, VIVO, the first ending and repeat were added by the composer in his recorded performance of LES CINQ DOIGTS mentioned above.

FOREWORD (continued)

VALSE AND POLKA

Composed at Clarens, Switzerland, in 1915.

This is an almost literal transcription of Nos. 2 and 3 from THREE EASY PIECES FOR PIANO DUET. Fortunately I was able to leave all the notes at their original posts without overtaxing the performer. The introductory bars to the VALSE and to the POLKA were not included in the original duets but were added later by the composer in his instrumental version (Suite No. 2 for small orchestra). The same applies to the dominant seventh arpeggio in the left hand at the close of the VALSE.

VALSE POUR LES ENFANTS (A Waltz for children)

Composed at Morges, Switzerland, in 1917 this short piece was subsequently published in the Paris daily newspaper *Le Figaro* on May 21, 1922. The caption read:

VALSE POUR LES ENFANTS
improvisée au Figaro par
IGOR STRAVINSKY

This wasn't to the liking of the composer who scribbled in French on a copy stored in his archives (I quote from memory): "Pas du tout improvisée, tout ce qu'il y a de plus composée! I. Str." (Translated: "Not improvised in the least, but quite thoroughly composed.")

FOUR ÉTUDES (Op. 7)

Composed at Oustiloug, Russia, in 1908.

1. (c minor)

The original metronome marking is ♩ = 88. The editor suggests ♩ = 80 on two counts: Firstly to allow the initial lyrical melody to soar in majesty and expression over its turbulent background. Secondly to prepare and control the typical dynamic buildup in the middle section.

2. (D major)

The editor's concern in this Étude was primarily the normalization and distribution of slurs over the right hand rhythmic patterns for a clearer understanding and an easier negotiation of their complex structure. Single beams have replaced the double beams in the left hand in measures 4–40 and 67–88.

3. (e minor)

In the original edition of this Étude an overall dynamic indication reads *"sempre con sord."*. However, performances of this piece have made me aware that the quality of the piano or the acoustics of the room often prove to be detrimental to the use of the damper throughout. Consequently I suggest *con sord., ad lib.*, preferring to leave the use of the soft pedal to the discretion of the performer.

4. (F# major)

Stravinsky gave me two important clues to the interpretation of this Étude. He insisted that the passage between measures 41 and 45 be played in a mellow tone "alla Chopin". He also advised me repeatedly to disregard his *cresc....* f in the last two measures and give them instead the opposite dynamic effect, (hence the *dim....* pp marked at this spot in the present edition).

—Soulima Stravinsky

PUBLISHER'S NOTE from *Stravinsky for Piano*

Souvenir d'une marche boche dates from 1915. The manuscript was reproduced in facsimile in *The Book of the Homeless* (*Le Livre des sans-foyer*), edited by Edith Wharton, published in London in 1916, and sold for the benefit of Belgian orphans.

The transcription of the **Chorus from the Prologue to 'Boris Godunov'** can be dated to August or September 1918 as it is to be found on the same page as one of the final sketches for *L'Histoire du soldat*. Stravinsky transposed Moussorgsky's chorus from F minor to A minor and added the metronome mark ♩ = 92. The words of the first line of the chorus, "Why have you forsaken us, our father?", were written (in Russian) by Stravinsky at the head of the manuscript. In the present edition square brackets indicate suggested dynamics, tempo indications and phrasing, by reference to Rimsky-Korsakov's edition of Moussorgsky's uncompleted opera. All other such markings are given as in Stravinsky's manuscript. Bars 8 to 14 of the ¾ section are problematic in that some of the accidentals in the manuscript are ambiguous or contradict the Rimsky-Korsakov edition. As the Rimsky-Korsakov and the Shostakovich editions of the opera agree on the harmony in this passage, it can only be presumed that, in haste, Stravinsky mistransposed certain harmony notes on account of the double transposition required of some wind parts in the full score. In this passage, the harmony has therefore been silently corrected according to the Rimsky-Korsakov edition.

The **Fragment** 'des symphonies pour instruments à vent à la mémoire de Achille-Claude Debussy' was originally published in a supplement to *La Revue musicale*, December 1920, entitled 'Tombeau de Claude Debussy'. That this piano reduction is devoid of dynamic markings suggests its being a 'memorial' intended to be read rather than performed, the homage paid by one master of the piano to another.

The publishers gratefully acknowledge the assistance of Mr. Robert Threlfall in the preparation of this publication.

Music origination by Jack Thompson.

(This page is left blank to facilitate page turns.)

Chant du Rossignol

1. La fête au palais de l'empereur de Chine

Edited by
ALBERT SPALDING
(New York)

IGOR STRAVINSKY

4

14

2. Les deux Rossignols

Toutes les doubles croches sont égales

Jeu du Rossignol mécanique

Modérato ♩ = 60

3. Maladie et guérison de l'empereur de Chine

26

(This page is left blank to facilitate page turns.)

Chorus from the Prologue to 'Boris Godunov'

Why have you forsaken us, our father?

Transcribed for piano solo by
IGOR STRAVINSKY
(1918)

MODESTE MOUSSORGSKY
(1839–1881)

(This page is left blank to facilitate page turns.)

Les cinq doigts

(The Five Fingers)

8 Easy tunes on 5 notes

Edited by
SOULIMA STRAVINSKY

IGOR STRAVINSKY

1. Andantino

40

2. Allegro

3. Allegretto

4. Larghetto

5. Moderato

6. Lento

*See Foreword

7. Vivo

sempre stacc.

p

*See Foreword

Fine

8. Pesante

Four Études

Edited by
SOULIMA STRAVINSKY

IGOR STRAVINSKY

1

2

60

3

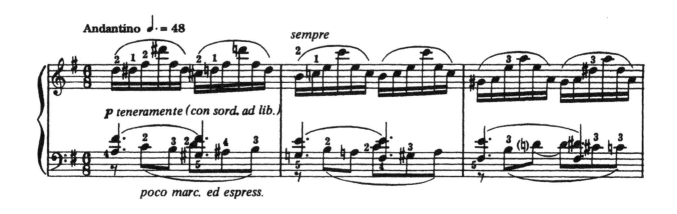

4

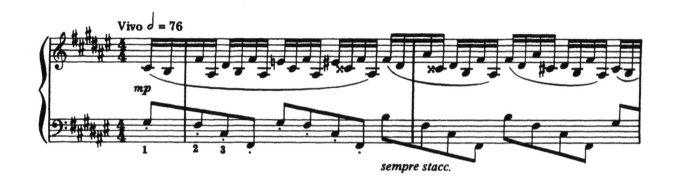

Fragment des symphonies pour instruments à vent à la mémoire de Achille-Claude Debussy

Piano Reduction by
IGOR STRAVINSKY
(1920)

(This page is left blank to facilitate page turns.)

To Arthur Rubinstein

Piano Rag-Music

Edited by
SOULIMA STRAVINSKY

IGOR STRAVINSKY

*The G♮s should be played with a very close legato, achieved by combining fingers and pedal.

To Sergei Diaghilev

Polka

Transcribed and edited by
SOULIMA STRAVINSKY

IGOR STRAVINSKY

*Grace notes occur before the beat.

To my wife

Serenade in A

Edited by
SOULIMA STRAVINSKY

Hymn

IGOR STRAVINSKY
(1925)

*All trills start on the note

*Depress without striking

Romanza

* Release key half way while retaining vibration

*All grace-notes before the beat

*Depress without striking

Rondoletto

* Depress without striking

Cadenza Finale

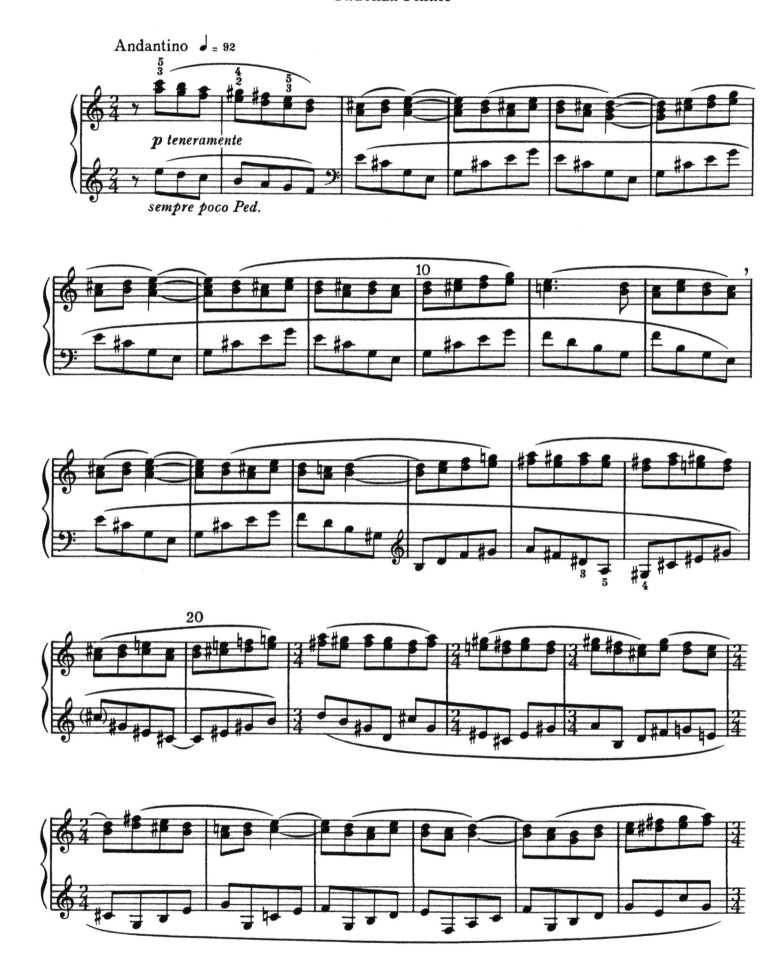

Dédiée à Madame la Princesse Edmond de POLIGNAC

Sonata

Edited by
ALBERT SPALDING
(New York)

1

IGOR STRAVINSKY
(1924)

articulato ma
non staccato

2

3

118

sub. *f* et détaché

più f sub.

Souvenir d'une marche boche

IGOR STRAVINSKY
(1915)

FINE

D. S. al Fine

Morges, 1 Sept. 1915

Tango

Edited by
SOULIMA STRAVINSKY

IGOR STRAVINSKY
(1925)

Arthur Rubinstein

Trois mouvements de Pétrouchka

1. Danse Russe

Transcribed for piano solo by
IGOR STRAVINSKY
(1911–1921)

Propriété de l'éditeur pour tous pays

Poco meno mosso

Tempo I (Allegro giusto)

2. Chez Pétrouchka

138

3. La semaine grasse

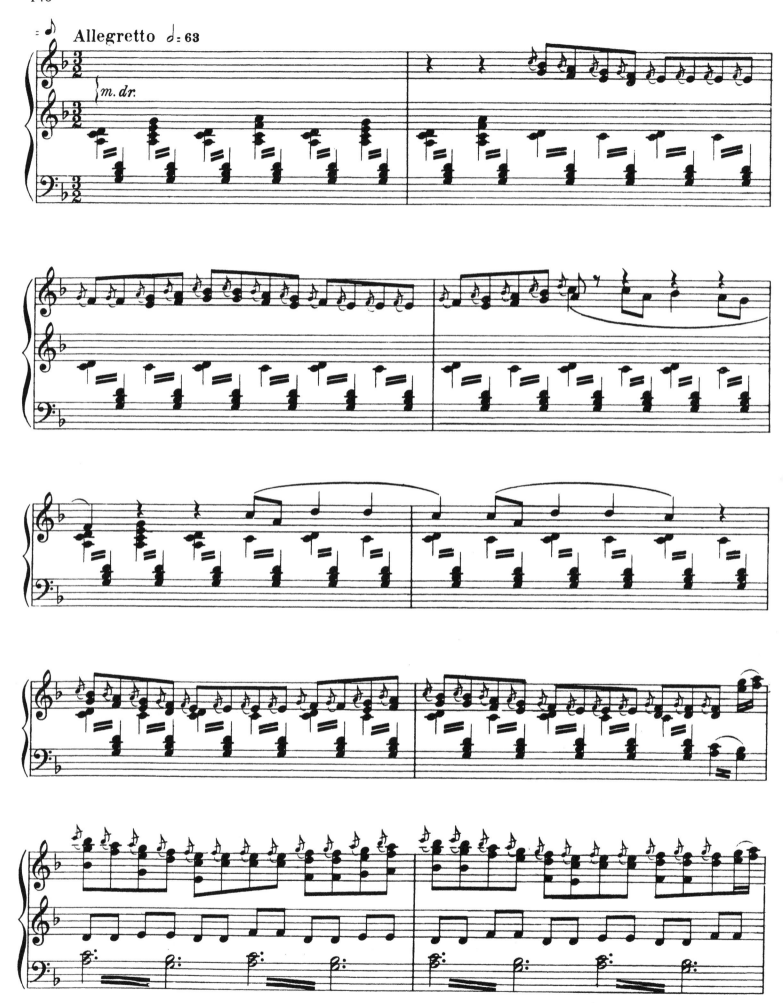

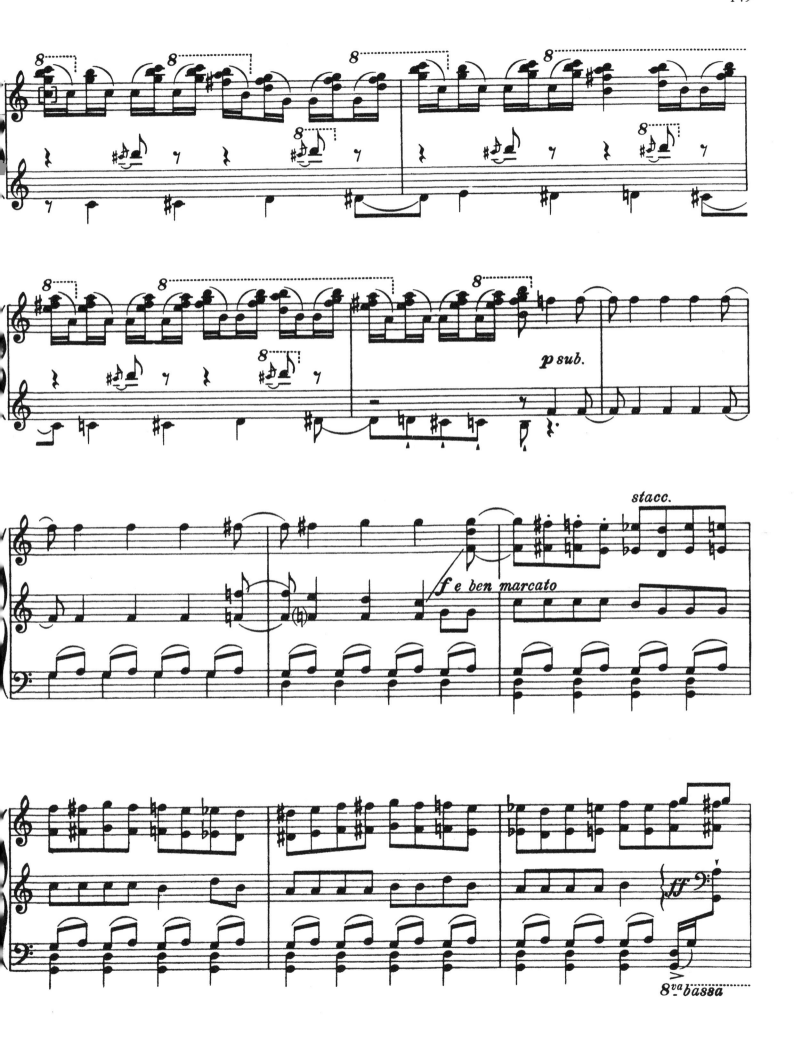

*) Sans changer le mouvement, la valeur de la ♪ étant la même que dans le 6/8 précédant. Le „Più mosso" n'est donc qu'une indication du caractère du mouvement par raport au précédant.

160

Anglet, 1921.

To Erik Satie

Valse

Transcribed and edited by
SOULIMA STRAVINSKY

IGOR STRAVINSKY

*Grace notes occur before the beat.

*Grace notes occur before the beat.

Valse pour les enfants

Edited by
SOULIMA STRAVINSKY

IGOR STRAVINSKY
(1917)